THE BATTLE FOR SURVIVAL

Written by Bettina Bird and Joan Short

Cover photograph: African elephants
Title page photograph: Leafy sea-dragon
Contents page photograph: Puma drinking, Arizona, U.S.A.

The Battle for Survival

©1994 By Bettina Bird and Joan Short
Illustrations by Rick Youmans
©1994 Photograph Credits:
    A.N.T. Photo Library:
    Cover shot: Silvestris
    Page 1, 18 (right). J Frazier; 2/3, 7, 15, 16, 19 (top right), 22, 23. NHPA;
    4, 8. Silvestris; 9. Ralph & Daphne Keller; 12. J. Carnemolla;
    13 (left). C & S Pollitt; 13 (right). S Wilson; 17 (left). Robert W. G. Jenkins;
    17 (right), 20 (right). Mark Wellard; 18 (left). Rudie H. Kuiter;
    19 (top left), 20 (left). Klaus Uhlenhut; 19 (bottom left). Andrew Dennis;
    19 (bottom right). R. Thwaites; 21 (2 shots). Otto Rogge;
    29. Ron & Valerie Taylor; 30. Pavel German.

©1994 Publisher: Pye Andersen Ltd

ISBN 0 435 00842 0 Pack 1
ISBN 0 435 00843 9 Group Pack

Created and designed by the Wendy Pye Team, New Zealand.

All rights reserved. No part of this publication may be reproduced or transmitted in any form or by any means, electronic or mechanical, including photocopy, recording or any information storage and retrieval system, without permission in writing from the publishers.

Heinemann Educational,
a Division of Heinemann Publishers (Oxford) Ltd,
Halley Court, Jordan Hill, Oxford OX2 8EJ

OXFORD LONDON EDINBURGH
MADRID ATHENS BOLOGNA PARIS
MELBOURNE SYDNEY AUCKLAND SINGAPORE
TOKYO IBADAN NAIROBI HARARE
GABORONE PORTSMOUTH NH (USA)

Printed by Colorcraft, Hong Kong.

98 97 96 95 94
10 9 8 7 6 5 4 3 2 1

Contents

The Battle for Survival 4
The Search for Food 5
The Search for Food in the
　　Underwater Environment 10
Water and Survival 12
The Sensing of Danger 14
Escaping from Predators 16
Extinct Animals – Losers in the
　　Battle for Survival 24
Conservation 29
We Can All Help 31
Glossary 32
Index .... Inside Back Cover

The Battle for Survival

On the land, in the air, and in the oceans, lakes and rivers, animals have an unending struggle to keep themselves and their young ones alive. They must find food and water, and they must develop ways to protect themselves and their young from enemies so that they can live. This struggle to stay alive is often called the "battle for survival". Species of animals that fail in the battle for survival become extinct.

Lions bringing down a buffalo to eat.

The Search For Food

Animals need food to survive. They eat many different kinds of food and have many different ways of getting it:

- **Animals that eat plants are called *herbivores*.**
  Plants contain vitamins and other foods that all animals need to keep them healthy. If there were no plants on Earth there would be no animals.

- **Animals that kill and eat other animals are called *carnivores*.**
  Carnivores get their vitamins "second-hand", from the meat of animals that eat plants.

- **Animals that eat plants and other animals are called *omnivores*.**
  Omnivores get their vitamins from plants and from the meat of animals they eat.

A gazelle is a herbivore.

A leopard is a carnivore.

An ostrich is an omnivore. (Ostriches usually eat plants, but they also eat lizards and tortoises.)

Herbivores

Herbivores eat plant foods such as grass, moss, lichen, leaves, flowers, berries, fruits, nuts and roots. Many, but not all, plant-eaters have sharp front teeth (called incisors) to bite off food, and large back teeth (called molars) to grind it. Some herbivores, such as rabbits, have extra incisors but no molars.

Kangaroos are herbivores

Kangaroos eat grass and shrubs. They can pick up, hold and lift food with their front paws. Kangaroos often use their front paws to hold the small branches of shrubs steady while they nibble the leaves.

A newborn kangaroo (or joey as it is called) is about the size of a peanut. From within its mother's pouch, a joey drinks its mother's milk and grows quickly. At about five months it puts its head out of the pouch and at seven months it can hop in and out. Even when a joey can eat grass it will continue to drink its mother's milk until it is about 18 months old.

A joey will sometimes eat grass from the safety of the mother's pouch.

Elephants are herbivores

Elephants eat grasses, shrubs, leaves, bark, branches, roots and water plants. Tusks are used to rip bark from trees and to dig up roots. The trunk is used to pick up food and to squirt water into the elephant's mouth. With its large, strong forehead, an elephant butts down small trees so that it can eat the top branches and leaves.

A female elephant and her calf.

Carnivores

Carnivores eat other animals. Animals that hunt and kill other animals for food are called predators. The animals that are being hunted are called the prey.

Most carnivores have good eyesight and hearing, and a good sense of smell. Some have sharp claws and teeth for catching, killing or eating their prey.

Cheetahs are carnivores

Hidden by long grass, a cheetah silently stalks its prey. When it is close enough, it springs out and gives chase. A cheetah can run at speeds of up to 110 kilometres per hour for a short time. Cheetahs are the fastest animals on earth.

Carnivores must kill to feed themselves. This cheetah closes in on a zebra in the African savannah.

Omnivores

Because omnivores eat plant foods as well as meat or fish, they have a good chance of survival. If prey is hard to find or catch, omnivores can still eat plants.

Brown rats are omnivores

Brown rats eat almost anything.
They steal birds' eggs.
They kill and eat baby rabbits.
They eat animals that are already dead and rotting.
They brave blackberry thorns to reach the fruit.

Brown rats are egg robbers.

Yellow-tailed black cockatoos are omnivores

Yellow-tailed black cockatoos use the claws of their four-toed feet to hold their food. With their strong curved beaks, they crack the hard seed pods of banksia bushes and casuarina trees and take out each seed. These cockatoos rip into rotting trees with their hooked beaks to reach wood-boring insect larvae. There is always a litter of bark and seed pods around a tree where yellow-tailed black cockatoos have been feeding.

Hooked beaks rip into rotting wood.

The Search for Food in the Underwater Environment

The brilliant red kelp snail is one sea creature that eats only plant food. These herbivores eat the surface stems of kelp.

Very few fish and other water creatures eat only plants. Many water creatures are omnivores. They eat (as well as water plants) worms, insect larvae, small fish, and the eggs and tiny young of other water creatures. However, most fish and other creatures of the rivers, lakes and oceans are carnivores.

Mosquito larvae – food for underwater omnivores.

Two types of ocean carnivores are the seals (which eat fish) and the great white sharks (which eat fish and seals).

Many water creatures live mainly on plankton. Plankton is the floating mass of very tiny water creatures and plants that drifts near the surface of oceans, lakes and rivers. Some of these tiny creatures and plants can be seen only through a microscope. Plant plankton is the basic source of vitamins for many water creatures.

Krill range from 10 millimetres to 150 millimetres in length.

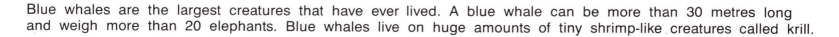

Blue whales are the largest creatures that have ever lived. A blue whale can be more than 30 metres long and weigh more than 20 elephants. Blue whales live on huge amounts of tiny shrimp-like creatures called krill.

Water and Survival

Most land animals and land-based birds, if they are to survive, need water to drink. But sometimes the simple task of getting a drink can be a matter of life and death. When an animal has its head down drinking, it is open to attack from predators.

Some animals get moisture from food and from dew.

The koala

The word "koala" is said to have come from an Aboriginal word that means the "animal that does not drink".

Koalas get most of their moisture from juicy, young leaves of various types of eucalyptus trees, and from dew. However, koalas seek out and drink water during very hot weather.

At a waterhole, giraffes always take turns to drink. Those not drinking keep a sharp look-out for danger. A lioness may be crouching in the scrub waiting to pounce on a young giraffe.

A koala eating eucalyptus (gumtree) leaves.

Water in the deserts

In the vast areas of deserts all over the world, animals develop a variety of very clever ways to survive when water is scarce.

Desert tortoises are able to make water from the food that they eat. They store this water in sacs under their shells. A full store of water (about two and a half cups) can last a tortoise throughout the entire dry season.

The Sensing of Danger

Many animals of prey have sharp senses of sight, hearing and smell to detect predators. Survival often relies on animals having an early warning system that alerts them to danger.

Rabbits use their senses to detect danger

A rabbit uses all three senses of sight, hearing and smell to detect if a predator is near.

A rabbit's eyes, like those of most animals of prey, are on each side of its head. Therefore, a rabbit can see danger to its right and left and in front of it. By turning its head quickly to the right or left, it can also see what is behind it. On looking up, it has a wide view of the sky, where a bird may be flying on the lookout for prey.

A rabbit can prick up and move its long, wide ears to trap any suspicious sounds. It can quickly judge the direction from which the sound is coming.

A rabbit has a sharp sense of smell. Its nose twitches as it sniffs the air for the scent of an approaching fox or some other predator.

Signalling danger

Like many other animals of prey, rabbits have special ways of signalling danger. When a rabbit senses danger, it may thump the ground with a hind foot. The sharp ears of the other rabbits pick up the sound and they are alerted to the danger.

As a frightened rabbit runs for the safety of its burrow (or zigzags across the ground in an attempt to confuse the enemy), the sharp eyes of other rabbits notice the fleeing rabbit's white tail bobbing up and down and they know that danger is nearby.

A white tail bobbing up and down signals danger.

Escaping from Predators

Most animals, once danger has been sensed, have ways of escaping or hiding from predators or ways of warning predators off. Predators do not always win.

- Some animals escape by using flight.

- Some animals escape by using camouflage or colour changes to deceive their predators.

- Some animals escape by using special colours to warn off attackers.

- Other animals have nasty surprises in store for their attackers.

Escaping predators by using flight

Most hoofed animals try to outrun their predators. All hoofed animals are herbivores and most live in herds. There is safety in numbers. It is usually old, sick or very young animals, which cannot keep up with the herd, that are caught.

When frightened, a herd of impala races away in leaps and bounds at great speed. Impala can outrun most predators, and the sight of so many leaping, bounding animals helps to confuse the enemy.

Green Tree Frog.

A frog's large, bulging eyes give it a wide view of what is happening around it. Its hearing is sharp. When alerted to danger through sight and hearing, most frogs use their strong, long back legs to leap for the safety of water or tall grass.

Many fish depend on swimming speed to escape from an enemy. One type of fish, the flying fish, takes to the air. Movements of its strong tail thrust it from the water. It uses its large fins as wings.

If an octopus sees an enemy, such as a shark, approaching, it squirts a black fluid into the water from a tube called a siphon. The siphon is just below the head. Hidden in clouds of black, inky fluid, the octopus makes its escape from the enemy.

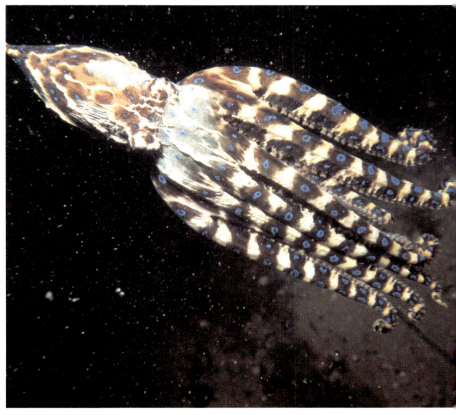

Blue-ringed Octopus.

17

Escaping predators by using camouflage

Instead of trying to escape from an enemy, some animals use camouflage to help them hide. By remaining quite still, the colour or shape of their bodies blends with the patterns of light and shade and the colours or shapes of things around them.

The sole merges with the colour patterns of the sea bed.

Two tawny frogmouth owls merge with the colour of the tree.

Escaping predators by changing colour

Some animals such as tree frogs can change the colour of their skin very quickly to match new surroundings.

Rock ptarmigans live in and near the Arctic. In winter, when their feathers are white the rock ptarmigans are almost invisible against the snow.

When this tree frog moved from one background to another, its skin changed colour to match the new surroundings.

In spring, when they moult the new feathers are speckly brown to match the summer vegetation around the ptarmigans' nests on the ground.

Escaping predators by using shape camouflage

Some animals use shape camouflage to help them hide. They look like parts of the plants in their surroundings, and predators often do not notice them.

Camouflage also helps some predators to remain hidden until the animals they are hunting are close enough to be attacked.

The stick insect resembles twigs.

Escaping predators by using warning colours

Many small animals use bright colours to warn predators to keep away. Some of these animals have a very nasty taste if bitten. Others have a poisonous bite or sting.

This small blue-ringed octopus blends with the colours of rocks in reefs and beach pools until it is disturbed. Then bright blue warning rings appear on its body and tentacles. Its bite is extremely poisonous and can be fatal for humans.

The cup-moth caterpillar has a nasty sting.

Once a predator has experienced the nasty taste or painful bite or sting of a brightly coloured animal, it recognizes the warning colour patterns when it comes across them again and leaves animals with those colourings alone.

The ladybird has a nasty taste if bitten.

Escaping predators by mimicking

Some harmless animals mimic the warning colours of a dangerous animal that lives in or near their own habitats. They do this to deter predators.

The eastern coral snake lives in the south-eastern parts of the United States of America. It is also known as the harlequin snake. Its bite is extremely poisonous. Bands of warning colours along its length run yellow-red-yellow-black, yellow-red-yellow-black and so on.

The harmless milk snake, which mimics the coral snake, has bands of the same three colours arranged in a different order. These bands run yellow-black-red-black, yellow-black-red and so on. Apparently, predators notice only the warning colours and not their order.

The false coral snake.

Nasty surprises

Some animals spray their enemies with a foul-smelling liquid or a poisonous gas.

The skunk is well known for the foul-smelling liquid that it sprays if it is attacked or annoyed. It first warns its attacker by stamping its front feet, and hissing and growling. If this has no effect, it lifts its furry tail in the air and squirts its foul spray on the enemy. The liquid comes from two glands just beneath its tail. Its aim can be accurate up to four metres away. The disgusting smell lasts for days on whatever has been hit. The fluid may also blind an animal for a short time. Animals, and humans too, learn to leave a skunk alone.

A skunk.

The millipede has a row of tiny holes along each side of its body. If attacked, it shoots a poisonous gas from these holes.

Extinct Animals – Losers in the Battle for Survival

In the distant past, many strange animals lived on the earth. Some were very small and others very large.

Over the ages many of these species lost the battle to survive. They became extinct. Today, we only know these animals existed because scientists have found their fossilized remains.

Fossils are the remains of plants or animals that lived in the past. For example, a fossil may be a bone, a tooth, or a shell hardened during long ages in the earth. A fossil can also be the imprint in rock of a footprint made in days long ago.

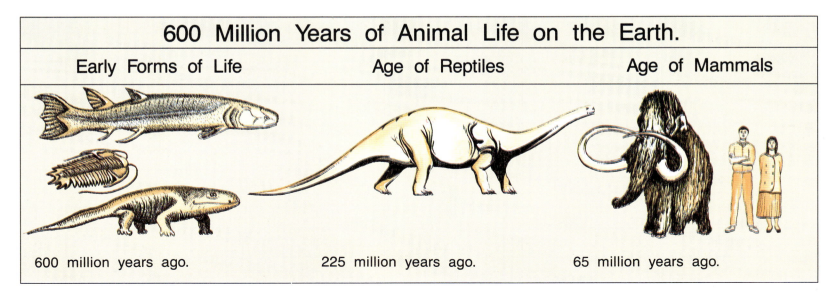

600 Million Years of Animal Life on the Earth.

Early Forms of Life	Age of Reptiles	Age of Mammals
600 million years ago.	225 million years ago.	65 million years ago.

600 million years of animal life on Earth

By using fossils, scientists have been able to work out how long animals have inhabited the earth. The oldest known animal fossils are about 600 million years old. At times, there were more of one type of animal than others. Over millions of years, as some types of animals were dying out, others were developing, and they took the place of those that became extinct. Today, we are in the Age of Mammals. Human beings are mammals.

The young of all mammals feed on their mother's milk. Some examples of present-day mammals are the monkeys, the tigers, the dolphins and humans.

Why extinction?

Scientists have suggested many reasons why animals of past ages became extinct. One reason may be that diseases caused them to die out. Another cause could be the great changes in weather world-wide. A change from warmth to bitter cold would have killed many plants. Plant-eating animals would then have starved and carnivores that fed on plant-eating animals would also have died.

World weather has changed many times over the ages. At the beginning of the Age of Mammals the weather warmed up, but later it became very cold for thousands of years. Ice and snow covered huge areas of the earth. Many species of animals died out because of cold and lack of food. Today, large areas around both the North and the South Pole remain covered with permanent ice.

Woolly mammoths became extinct about 10,000 years ago. Long before that time, some mammoths became trapped in a deep crevasse in icy Eastern Siberia. Their bodies are still in the crevasse today, frozen solid. They are fossils preserved in permanent ice.

An extinct mammal – the woolly mammoth.

The sabre-toothed tiger — an extinct mammal.

Why did dinosaurs become extinct?

The time of the dinosaurs may have ended when a huge meteorite hit the earth and threw so much dust and debris into the atmosphere that day became night and the temperature cooled too rapidly for the dinosaurs to survive. No one knows for certain why the dinosaurs became extinct but it must have been a terrible thing to destroy such a successful species.

Humans and extinction

During the Age of Mammals, when humans first appeared on the Earth they hunted animals for their warm, furry skins and for food. Many scientists think that the activities of humans contributed to the extinction of some species of animals in those far-off times. But what about more recent times?

In the 1600s, humans caused a flightless bird called the dodo to become extinct. The dodo lived on the island of Mauritius. European sailors often called at Mauritius and killed the birds for food. Rats and dogs that came in the sailing ships ate the eggs of the dodo. By 1681, the dodo was extinct.

Over 100 years ago, there were many marsupial wolves on the Australian island of Tasmania. Because these animals had dark stripes across the rear of their backs, they were usually called Tasmanian tigers.

These animals preyed on the European settlers' sheep and poultry, and so they were hunted. The last-known Tasmanian tiger died in the Hobart Zoo in 1936.

The dodo

The Tasmanian tiger

28

Conservation

These days, people are concerned because so many species of animals around the world are faced with extinction. But why are these animals endangered? Is anything being done to save them from extinction?

The threat of extinction to animals today

Many land animals and birds are threatened because their natural habitats are being destroyed as people drain wetlands and clear forests to grow crops, to obtain timber, or even to build large holiday resorts. When an animal's natural habitat is destroyed, that animal cannot find food or raise its young and the species becomes extinct.

Right whales (along with many other members of the whale family) were almost hunted to extinction by whale hunters.

Some water creatures are threatened with extinction by the pollution of rivers, lakes and oceans, and by over-fishing. It is only the recent campaigns by people against whale hunting that has saved many species of whales from extinction.

How zoos help to save rare animals

Many zoos now try to make the enclosures or open areas in which their animals live, a copy of each animal's natural habitat. This encourages the animals to breed. Zoos organize breeding programmes in the hope that there will always be young animals to carry on the species. This applies particularly to animals that are in danger of extinction. Many young animals bred in zoos are re-established in wildlife reserves in their natural homelands.

Taronga Zoo in Australia is the only zoo in the world to display and breed the Fijian crested iguana, a rare and beautiful reptile. The reptile staff at the zoo keep in close contact with Fiji about the iguanas' welfare.

We Can All Help

For many endangered species, like the giant panda and the African elephant, time is running out. All over the world, people are now working together to protect endangered animals and their habitats, before they disappear from the Earth forever.

Finding out about the animals that live in the world around us is the first step towards saving endangered species. Here are some more ways you can help with conservation:

- Don't buy things that are made from endangered species. For example ivory, tortoiseshell and wild animal skins.

- Use biodegradable products that won't pollute the habitats of wildlife.

- Don't waste paper. Paper is made from trees, which may be the homes of animals. You can recycle paper, too.

- Be careful not to damage plants when you walk through the countryside. You could easily destroy an animal's habitat.

- Spread the word. Tell your friends and family about conservation.

- Find out more about conservation by writing to organisations such as:

Greenpeace, Canonbury Villas, London N1 2PN.

World Wide Fund For Nature, Panda House, Wayside Park, Godalming, Surrey GU7 1XR

Friends of the Earth, 26-28 Underwood Street, London N1 7JQ.

Glossary

Banksia   An Australian plant with dense spikes of flowers.

Camouflage   A disguise that blends in with the surroundings.

Carnivores   Flesh-eating animals or plants.

Casuarina   A kind of Australian tree with branches that look like large horse-tails.

Habitat   The place where a plant or animal usually lives.

Herbivores   Animals that eat plants.

Marsupial   A kind of animal in which the female carries its young in a pouch.

Omnivores   Animals that eat plants and other animals.

Predator   An animal that kills other animals for food.

Species   A group of animals or plants which has some characteristics in common.